Text copyright © 2001 Jean Watson
Photographs copyright © 2001 Leonard Smith
This edition copyright © 2001 Lion Publishing

The moral rights of the author and photographer
have been asserted

Published by
Lion Publishing plc
Sandy Lane West, Oxford, England
www.lion-publishing.co.uk
ISBN 0 7459 4724 7

First edition 2001
1 3 5 7 9 10 8 6 4 2 0

Acknowledgments

11, 14, 19, 26, 30: I Timothy 6:17; Genesis 2:8, 15;
Psalm 104:14–15; Psalm 90:2; Genesis 2:9, taken
from the *Holy Bible, New International Version*, copyright
© 1973, 1978, 1984 by International Bible Society.
Used by permission.

33: taken from 'Vegetation' by Kathleen Raine, used by
permission of Anthroposophic Press & Lindisfarne Books.

A catalogue record for this book is available
from the British Library

Typeset in Venetian 301
Printed and bound in Singapore

Gardens
Thoughts to inspire

WRITTEN AND COMPILED BY JEAN WATSON
PHOTOGRAPHY BY LEONARD SMITH

LION
Giftlines

Contents

Introduction

My husband loved working in our garden, and, thanks to him, I loved just *being* in it!

His sudden death brought many changes, not least because I had to take a more active role in making the garden grow. More than this, my grief drew me to gardens and the world of nature in a new and profound way.

Now, more than ever, I need what these can offer. Beauty to delight. Complexity to wonder at. Peace and continuity to restore and comfort. New growth to foster hope.

I write as an enthusiastic appreciator and apprentice, and I hope that, in a small way, the thoughts and quotations in this book will say something about the capacity of gardens and gardening to influence our lives.

Jean Watson

Why Does Your Garden Grow?

If you have a garden, what does it mean to you? A garden can be a private joy or a place for entertaining friends; a workshop or a work of art; an arena for self-expression or a place to play and relax in; a memorial to a loved and honoured person or a place created to commemorate the end of war.

It can be just a few window boxes, a large public park, or any size in between. As their potential for attracting, healing and comforting is increasingly recognized, gardens are being built in new places: around — or even on top of — hospitals, hospices and shops.

I sat in a beautiful garden,
Dreaming away the hours;
Bathed in the golden sunlight,
Charmed by the scent of flowers.

Author unknown

This world of God's is a wonderful place –
with mighty things like mountains; and
things of delicate workmanship like
cartwheel spiders' webs spangled with
diamond dew; and things wonderfully
put together – tiny shells in pools, and
birds' nests in spring; and colourful things –
clouds silver in the blue sky, and leaves scarlet and
gold in autumn, and hues brighter than any paint box
when the sun goes down.

Rita Snowden

Mary, Mary, quite contrary,
How does your garden grow?
With silver bells and cockle shells
And pretty maids all in a row.

Traditional English rhyme

God richly provides
us with everything
for our enjoyment.

From the New Testament

Inspired Work

Gardening involves expertise and a whole range of skills. A knowledge of plants, soil and weather conditions. An understanding of the principles of good growth and the strength and skill to carry them out. The ability to use manual and mechanical tools for mowing, cutting, pruning, digging, trenching, hoeing, planting, potting, weeding and staking. To true gardeners, their work is a labour of loving creativity; and gardens have also proved an inspiring subject for numerous writers and artists.

Long live the weeds
and the wilderness yet.

Gerard Manley Hopkins

The Lord God had planted a garden in the east,
in Eden; and there he put the man he had formed.
The Lord God took the man and put him in the
Garden of Eden to work it and take care of it.

From the Old Testament

Half a proper gardener's work is done upon his knees.

Rudyard Kipling

Gardening is
an active
participation
in the deepest
mysteries of the
universe.

Thomas Berry

Plants to Sustain

I have found it fascinating to browse through a book on food plants and be reminded of their range and variety. There are crops that provide grain, sugar, oil, nuts, vegetables, fruit, herbs, spices and flavourings, mushrooms, truffles and drinks.

What would we do, for example, without the grass family from which most of the grain crops come and which are so vital for feeding people and livestock? And not only the different varieties of wheat, but rye, oats, barley, maize, corn, rice and millets!

Oats and beans and barley grow –
Nor you nor I nor anyone knows
How oats and beans and barley grow.

Traditional English rhyme

Nothing we see, but

means our good,

As our delight, or

as our treasure:

The whole is, either

our cupboard of food,

Or cabinet of pleasure.

George Herbert

He makes grass grow for
the cattle, and plants
for man to cultivate —
bringing forth food
from the earth: wine
that gladdens the heart
of man, oil to make his
face shine, and bread
that sustains his heart.

From the Old Testament

Lovely as a Tree

Trees have not always been regarded as lovely. Forests used to be associated with wildness and danger, and open country was thought to be safer. 'Progress' and 'civilization' involved cutting down trees. Now, increasingly, trees are valued, planted, protected — for their beauty as well as for their usefulness.

They have always been a major source of inspiration for artists, poets and writers. William Blake wrote in 1799: 'The tree which moves some to tears of joy is in the Eyes of others only a Green thing that stands in the way. But to the Eyes of the Man of Imagination, Nature is Imagination itself.'

I think that I shall never see
A poem lovely as a tree.

Alfred Joyce Kilmer

Who has seen the wind?
Neither you nor I:
But when the trees bow down their heads,
The wind is passing by.

Christina Rossetti

God Almighty first planted a garden; and,
indeed, it is the purest of human pleasures.

Francis Bacon

Is it the lumberman who is the friend and lover
of the pine, stands nearest to it and understands
its nature best? No, no, it is the poet who makes
the truest use of the pine. It is the poet who loves
it as his own shadow in the air, and lets it stand.

Henry David Thoreau

Lasting as a Tree

Trees symbolize stability. They're always there — or nearly always. We had a gigantic flowering cherry in our garden. Its clouds of blossom lifted our spirits year after year. But one day, felled by hurricane winds, it had gone, leaving an empty space in the sky. Had we fully appreciated it while we had it? Probably not. However, in the absence of hurricanes and diseases, trees are solidly and reliably with us for generation after generation. Only the creator of the universe could outlast the oldest tree.

Among all the varying
productions with which
Nature has adorned
the surface of the earth,
none awakens our
sympathies, or interests
our imagination so
powerfully as those
venerable trees which
seem to have stood
the lapse of ages.

John Muir

Before the mountains were born or
you brought forth the earth and the world,
from everlasting to everlasting you are God.

From the Old Testament

Generations pass
while some tree
stands, and old
families last not
three oaks.

Sir Thomas Browne

There is a serene and settled majesty to woodland scenery that enters into the soul and delights and elevates it, and fills it with noble inclinations.

Washington Irving

Trees of Life

Trees are not only beautiful, but crucial to the environment. They hold up mountains and soften the effects of wind, storm and flood; they conserve water and provide shade, shelter and nourishment for all kinds of living creatures; from them we derive building materials, fuel, medicine, and a host of other things.

It strikes me that they are useful by simply being themselves. Isn't the same true of us? Putting on a show, trying to live up to our own or other people's unrealistic expectations, taking on something for which we are unsuited — what's the point? Ultimately, for good or ill, all we can ever truly be, offer or contribute, springs from who we really are.

I read, and sigh, and
wish I were a tree —
For sure then
I should grow...

George Herbert

The Lord God made all
kinds of trees grow out
of the ground — trees that
were pleasing to the eye
and good for food.

From the Old Testament

There was a bird upon the nest,
The finest bird you ever did see,
And the bird was on the nest,
And the nest was on the leaf,
And the leaf was on the twig,
And the twig was on the branch,
And the branch was on the bough,
And the bough was on the tree,
And the tree was on the hill,
And the hill stood still.
And the green grass grew
all around, all around,
And the green grass grew all around.

Traditional English rhyme

The World of Green

We all know far more these days about the intricate webs of
interconnectedness and interdependence within nature,
and hence the chain of effects for good or ill
that we set off by our lifestyle and actions.
I asked an ecologist what someone
like me could do to keep the environment
as healthy as possible for us and our
descendants. A few suggestions he gave
were: Make your own compost, but don't
use peat, which is the habitat for a whole range
of animals and plants. Let nettles grow on the edges of
your garden so that you support helpful, greenfly-eating insects
such as ladybirds. Encourage hedgehogs, who will kindly eat your
slugs. Put up nest boxes for birds.

O never harm the dreaming world,
the world of green, the world of leaves.

Kathleen Raine

What is green?

The grass is green,

With small flowers

between.

Christina Rossetti

Our bodies
are our gardens,
to the which our
wills are gardeners.

William Shakespeare

All nature has a feeling:
woods, fields, brooks
Are life eternal.

John Clare

Attitudes affect our actions. Wanting to respond creatively to all the loveliness and lushness, the fascination and fertility around us is half the battle.

Delight in Nature

Then, if we use our imaginations and exert ourselves, all of us — gardeners, environmentalists, tree surgeons, scientists, poets, artists, walkers, climbers, swimmers, flower arrangers, appreciators — can find ways of going about our daily lives that feel good and are good for us and our environment, both now and in the future; ways of taking care of, working with and celebrating the magnificence by which we are surrounded.

Oh! never
may we lose,
Dear friend!
our fresh delight
in simplest
nature's hues!

Felicia Dorothea Hemans

Familiarity with nature never breeds contempt.
The more one learns, the more he expects surprises,
and the more he becomes aware of the inscrutable.

Archibald Rutledge

Read Nature;
Nature is a friend to truth.

Edward Young

Beauty seen is never lost,
God's colours all are fast;
The glory of this sunset heaven
Into my soul has passed.

John Greenleaf Whittier

Echoes from Eternity

Philip Toynbee wrote in End of Journey: 'I am constantly aware that there is another reality which interpenetrates our own.' So am I. Do you know what I mean when I speak of those 'Ah!' moments in life? Times when tears spring to the eyes, or the skin prickles, or the scalp tingles with a kind of awed joy because something so impossibly, out-of-this-world good, right, special, happens and you know, feel, sense, that you are on holy ground, almost brushed by the wings of a passing angel.

It could be argued that this is just an aesthetic experience, but I think it goes beyond that. And these echoes from eternity, as I think of them, come to me not least when I am in tune with nature.

We don't need to be mystics to meet God
in the things he's made, or in ourselves.

Rowland Croucher

The world is
aflame with things
of eternal moment.

E. Margaret Clarkson

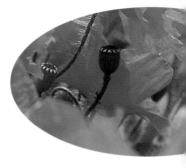

To see a World in a Grain of Sand,
And a Heaven in a Wild Flower,
Hold Infinity in the palm of your hand,
And Eternity in an hour.

William Blake

Leonard Smith

biographical details

Leonard Smith is an accomplished British photographer with eighteen years' experience. Wide acclaim of the work he produced at the age of eighteen, during a seven-week expedition to Greenland, encouraged him to turn professional. He is best known for his observational and opportunistic-style photographs, taken under controlled natural daylight and published both as a series of popular greetings cards and within editorial features. His card range sells throughout the United Kingdom, Europe, Australia and the Americas. Inspired by his Christian faith, Leonard seeks to capture the joy and wonder of the natural world; and a second side of his work is designed to promote thought, discussion and education. Working again with controlled natural daylight, Leonard captures poignant and unforgettable images of people and social environments. He travels widely on assignments in Africa and Asia, and frequently undertakes commissions for charitable organizations.

He is managing director of The Lens Ideas Studio, a publishing business he founded in May 1985. He lives in Suffolk, and is married with two young children.